STONE CIRCLE STORIES:
CULTURE AND FOLKTALES

CAUTIONARY STORIES

**BY
VIRGINIA
LOH-HAGAN**

People have been telling stories since the beginning of time. This series focuses on stories found across cultures. You may have heard these stories from your parents or grandparents. Or you may have told one yourself around a campfire. Stories explain the world around us. They inspire. They motivate. They even scare! We tell stories to share our history.

45th Parallel Press

Published in the United States of America by Cherry Lake Publishing
Ann Arbor, Michigan
www.cherrylakepublishing.com

Reading Adviser: Marla Conn MS, Ed., Literacy specialist, Read-Ability, Inc.
Book Designer: Jen Wahi

Photo Credits: ©durantelallera/Shutterstock.com, 5; ©mubus7/Shutterstock.com, 7; ©Boxyart/Shutterstock.com, 8; ©Damien Richard/Shutterstock.com, 11; ©Everett Historical/Shutterstock.com, 13; ©Debbie Steinhausser/Shutterstock.com, 14; ©JeremyRichards/Shutterstock.com, 17; ©Joe West/Shutterstock.com, 19; ©Fer Gregory/Shutterstock.com, 21; ©answer5/Shutterstock.com, 23; ©ZDL/Shutterstock.com, 25; ©Candace Hinton/Shutterstock.com, 27; ©Arieliona/Shutterstock.com, 28; ©andreiuc88/Shutterstock.com, cover and interior; Various grunge/texture patterns throughout courtesy of Shutterstock.com

45th Parallel Press is an imprint of Cherry Lake Publishing.

Library of Congress Cataloging-in-Publication Data has been filed and is available at catalog.loc.gov

Printed in the United States of America
Corporate Graphics

Aug 19
J
398.25

ABOUT THE AUTHOR:

Dr. Virginia Loh-Hagan is an author, university professor, and former classroom teacher. She is typing this story with broken thumbs. Her life right now is a cautionary tale! Make sure to use your tech devices properly. She lives in San Diego with her very tall husband and very naughty dogs. To learn more about her, visit www.virginialoh.com.

TABLE OF CONTENTS

CAUTIONARY STORIES

What are cautionary stories?
What is the purpose of cautionary stories?

Cautionary stories are warnings. They warn others of danger. They teach **morals**. Morals are lessons. Characters in these stories ignore rules. Characters suffer **consequences** because they don't listen. Consequences are punishments or effects.

Cautionary stories are often scary. They're told to children. Adults want children to follow rules. They want children to have good manners. They want to protect children. They want to keep children safe.

Cautionary tales are often spread by word of mouth.

Fables and **urban legends** are cautionary stories. Fables are short stories. They often have animals as main characters. Urban means city. Legends are stories. Urban legends are modern stories. They're like rumors about people or places.

CHAPTER 1

GIRL WITH THE RIBBON

Why did the girl wear the ribbon?
What rule did Johnny break?
What lesson did Johnny learn?

Jane wore a ribbon around her neck. She wore this ribbon every day. She never took it off. She even wore it in the shower!

Johnny lived next to Jane. He and Jane grew up together. They were best friends. As kids, Johnny didn't notice the ribbon.

There are several versions of this story. The girl's ribbon is sometimes a different color

Jane and Johnny became teens. Johnny asked, "Why do you wear that ribbon around your neck?" He asked her every day. Jane never answered him. She changed the topic.

Johnny liked Jane. He asked her out on dates. Johnny and Jane hung out a lot. They went out to eat. They watched movies. They went to school dances. Jane always wore her ribbon.

Johnny said, "You still haven't told me why you wear the ribbon." He asked her about it every day. Jane said, "One

Jane's ribbon is commonly shown as yellow. Yellow is a warning color.

SPOTLIGHT BIOGRAPHY

A famous cautionary tale is "Little Red Riding Hood." This story warns children of talking to strangers. It warns young girls to stay away from bad men. It's written by Charles Perrault. Perrault was a French writer. He said, "Children, especially attractive, well-bred young ladies, should never talk to strangers. For if they should do so, they may well provide dinner for a wolf." Wolves represent bad men. Perrault lived from 1628 to 1703. He was born in Paris. His family was rich. Perrault studied law. He worked in government jobs. He stopped working at age 67. He started writing children's stories. He was one of the first to write fairy tales. He also wrote "Cinderella," "Puss in Boots," "Sleeping Beauty," and "Bluebeard." He wrote these stories to amuse his grandchildren.

day, I'll tell you about it. But you'll be sorry." Johnny was annoyed. But he loved Jane. He accepted her answer.

When they became adults, Johnny **proposed**. Proposed means to ask to marry. Jane said yes. On their wedding night, Johnny asked about the ribbon. Jane said, "Does it really matter? You'll be sorry." Johnny thought about it.

He'd love her no matter what. He said, "You're right. It doesn't matter." Jane said, "If you want us to be happy together, you can never ask me about my ribbon again." Johnny agreed.

Johnny and Jane had 4 children. The children asked Jane about her ribbon. Johnny told them to not ask her about it.

Johnny became an old man. He asked Jane about the ribbon. Jane was sad. She said, "If you really want to know, you can untie my ribbon. But if you want us to be happy together, then you won't ask me again."

Johnny said, "You've made me very happy. But I've waited a long time. I need to know."

He pulled the ribbon. Jane's head fell off. She said, "I told you. Your **curiosity** killed our happiness." Curiosity is the need to know something. Jane died. Johnny was sorry.

A popular saying is "curiosity killed the cat."

CHAPTER 2

BRER BEAR AND BRER SKUNK

How did Brer Skunk trick Brer Bear?
What lesson did Brer Bear learn?

There are many stories about **Brer** Rabbit and his friends. Brer means brother. These stories come from Africa. Brer Bear was one friend.

Brer Bear had the biggest house. He had the biggest wife. He had the biggest children. Brer Bear's family did everything together. They played together. They hunted together. They ate together. They slept together. At night, they crawled into their big bed. But they were too fat. They didn't fit on the bed. Plus, they

African slaves brought these stories to the United States.

had too much stuff in their house. They didn't have any room to walk around. But they were warm.

One night, there was knocking on the door. This woke up Brer Bear's family. Brer Bear said, "Who is it?"

Brer Skunk said, "It's me. It's Brer Skunk."

Brer Bear said, "It's really late. We're sleeping. What do you want?"

Brer Skunk is a trickster.
Tricksters play tricks and fool others.

Brer Skunk said, "Winter is coming. It's really cold. Can I come in?"

Brer Bear looked around his messy house. He said, "No. We have no room."

Brer Skunk said, "But you have the biggest house."

Brer Bear said, "We have too much stuff. There's no room for you."

Brer Skunk wasn't going to quit. He said, "That's why you need me! I can clean for you. I'm a really good **housekeeper.**" Housekeepers clean houses as a job.

Brer Bear was really **cheap**. Cheap means not wanting to spend money. Brer Bear said, "I don't want to pay you."

FAST-FORWARD TO MODERN TIMES

There are many cautionary tales about eating fast food. Eating too much fast food is bad for people's health. But fast food tastes good. It's also easier than cooking. Today's kids are eating more fast food. Parents may try to get them to stop. There are stories being spread on the internet. People said burgers were made from worms. People said burgers were made out of dogs or horses. People said they found a finger in a cup of chili. People said milkshakes were made of animal fat. People said scientists were creating chickens without beaks, feet, or feathers. People said there was a rat tail in a chicken nugget. These stories were found to be false.

Brer Skunk said, "It's okay. I'll clean if you let me sleep over."

Brer Bear's family liked the idea. They needed their house cleaned. They nodded their heads. Brer Bear said, "Okay. You can stay. But you have to work first."

Brer Skunk said, "It's a deal!"

Brer Bear let Brer Skunk in. Brer Skunk came in. He looked around. He was happy to be warm. He turned around. He lifted his tail. He blasted the air with a bad smell. Then, he laughed.

Brer Bear and his family ran away. They were mad. Brer Bear said, "That skunk tricked us. We should've known better. Nothing is free."

Brer Skunk said, "Now, there's plenty of room." He fell asleep.

Skunks can spray up to 15 feet (4.6 meters).

CHAPTER 3

NIGHT MARCHERS

What are Night Marchers?
What are the rules for Night Marchers?
What happens when people break the rules?

There was a maid walking home one night. It was a foggy night. The maid saw ghosts marching toward her. She died the next day. Then, a man saw her ghost and other ghosts. They were marching on the beach. The next day, that man died.

This happened in Hawaii. Hawaii is a state in the United States. Imagine being on a Hawaiian beach at night. There's a full moon. There's a cool breeze.

Hawaii is a group of islands.
It's in the Pacific Ocean.

Drums can be heard. There's a smell of rotting meat. Bright torches light up the beach. Ghosts are holding the torches. These ghosts are **ancient** Hawaiian **warriors**. Ancient means from a long time ago. Warriors are

CROSS-CULTURAL CONNECTION

Heinrich Hoffmann was a German psychiatrist and writer. He wrote a famous book of cautionary tales. He did this in 1845. His book was the first to combine pictures and words. It was one of the first comic books. Hoffmann's stories were violent. They were scary. One story is about Conrad. Conrad sucks his thumbs. His mother tells him to stop. She said, "But mind now, Conrad, what I say. Don't suck your thumb while I'm away." She warns him about a tailor who cuts off thumbs. She says thumbs don't grow back. She leaves the house. Conrad doesn't listen. He doesn't believe her. He sucks his thumbs. Then, a tailor shows up. He has scissors in each of his hands. He chases Conrad. He cuts off Conrad's thumbs.

fighters. These ghosts are called *Huaka'I po*. This means Night Marchers.

Night Marchers protect the islands. They protect chiefs and other important people. They rise from their

burial sites. Burial sites are places where dead bodies are put. Some Night Marchers rise up from the ocean.

Night Marchers walk on air. They march together. They visit battle sites. They visit temples. They leave no trace. They march at night. They march through any **obstacle**. Obstacles are things that block a path. Nothing stops the Night Watchers. Nothing stands in their way.

Some Night Marchers come to take a dying family member to the ghost world.

Night Marchers are dressed for war. They carry weapons. They chant. They beat war drums. The drums let people know they're coming. They tell people to run and hide.

People can't look at the Night Marchers. People must lay unclothed on the floor. They must face the ground. They can't move. They can't interrupt the march. They must show respect.

If people don't listen, then bad things happen. Night Marchers kill people who don't follow rules. They set people on fire. Bolts of light and heat come out of their eyes. People's bodies turn into ashes. Then, they're forced to march with them forever.

There are 3 ways people can save themselves. First, they can pee on themselves. Second, they can plant a special plant. Third, they can be a Night Marcher's family member.

Many Hawaiians warn visitors to stay away from certain places at night, especially when alone! They say these sites are Night Marcher trails.

CHAPTER 4

HOOKMAN

Who is the Hookman?
Who does the Hookman attack?
What lesson is the Hookman teaching?

Hookman was a killer. He didn't have a hand. He had a hook instead. His hook was sharp.

Hookman escaped. Some stories say he escaped from prison. This makes him a criminal. Some stories say he escaped from a mental hospital. This makes him mentally ill.

Hookman was a serial killer.
Serial means repeating.

Hookman targeted women. He followed them. He
found their cars. He hid under their cars. He waited.
The women would walk to their cars. Hookman
attacked their ankles. He used his hook. He pulled their
bodies under the car. He killed them. This story scares

women. This story encourages women to protect themselves. They check under their cars. They look for Hookman.

Hookman also likes to attack teens who don't listen to their parents. There's a story about 2 teens who were dating. They lied to their parents. They said they were going to the movies. Instead, they went to Lovers' Lane. This is where teens go to kiss.

They listened to the radio. There was a special news report. There was a warning about a killer with a hook.

The teens heard a sound. It was a scraping sound on the car. The girl got scared. She said, "I want to go home." The boy said, "Don't worry. It's just the wind."

But the teens kept hearing strange sounds. They got scared. They left in a hurry.

Some stories say Hookman wears a long coat.

The boy took the girl home. They were in her driveway. They got out of the car. They looked at the door handle. They screamed. They saw a hook. The hook was hanging on the handle. The hook was bloody. It was ripped from a body. The girl said, "We should listen to our parents from now on."

Hookman scares people. He punishes teens for breaking rules. He punishes them for lying.

No one knows how Hookman lost his hand.

DID YOU KNOW?

- Teens like to test rules. They use cautionary tales as dares. This is called legend tripping. For example, haunted house stories are meant to keep people away. But teens dare each other to visit haunted houses. Teens may think they're more adult by taking dares.

- Social guidance movies are like cautionary tales. They're used in schools. They're educational. They teach lessons. An example is movies about the dangers of drugs.

- Many scary movies have teens in them. Scary movies are like cautionary tales. Teens do bad things. A killer attacks them. This warns teens to behave.

- Hilaire Belloc was an English writer. He's famous for writing cautionary tales for children. He had interesting titles for his stories. One title was Jim, who ran away from his nurse and was eaten by a lion. Another title was Matilda, who told lies and was burned to death.

CHALLENGE:

· ·

WRITE YOUR OWN TALE

BEFORE YOU WRITE:

❥ Read fables and urban legends. Use them as models.

❥ Make a list of lessons. Choose one to focus your story around.

❥ Think about the mistakes you've made. Think about lessons you've learned. Make a list. Use your own life to connect with readers.

❥ Complete a cause-and-effect story map. Think about actions. Think about consequences.

AS YOU WRITE:

❥ Keep the stories short. Don't bore readers before getting to the lesson.

❥ Create a villain. Villains are bad guys. They can be monsters. They can be killers.

❥ Create a main character. The main characters are regular people.

❥ Create a problem. Make the main character break a rule.

❥ Put the main character in danger. Create drama. Create a sense of fear.

❥ Describe the lesson. The general idea is that following rules is good and breaking rules is bad.

❥ Keep the setting and names vague. Vague means not clear. The idea is that the story could happen to anyone.

❥ Treat the story like it's true. Scary stories are scary because people think they could happen.

AFTER YOU WRITE:

❥ Proofread and edit your cautionary tale.

❥ Check to see if you used sensory details during the danger part. Sensory details include sight, touch, hearing, smell, and taste. These will increase the fear and drama.

❥ Share it with others. Tell it out loud. Add more details each time.

❥ Tell your cautionary tale to someone who needs a lesson. If you tell it to younger children, make sure it's appropriate.

CONSIDER THIS!

TAKE A POSITION! Some cautionary tales are really scary. They're violent. They're bloody. Do you think they should be told to children? Argue your point with reasons and evidence.

SAY WHAT? Read the 45th Parallel Press books about urban legends. Explain how they're cautionary tales. Explain the lessons.

THINK ABOUT IT! Why would parents tell cautionary tales? Think about your own parents. What are some of their worries? Do they tell you any cautionary tales? Do they try to teach you lessons?

LEARN MORE!

Caution: These may contain scary tales.

Belloc, Hilaire. *Cautionary Tales & Bad Child's Book of Beasts*. Mineola, NY: Dover Publications, 2008.

Ibbotson, Eva. *Let Sleeping Sea-Monsters Lie ... and Other Cautionary Tales*. London: Macmillan Children's Books, 2012.

Symons, Mitchell. *Happily Never After: Modern Cautionary Tales*. London: Doubleday Childrens, 2013.

GLOSSARY

ancient (AYN-shuhnt) from a long time ago

brer (BRAIR) brother

burial sites (BER-ee-uhl SITES) places where dead bodies are buried

cautionary (KAW-shuhn-er-ee) acting as a warning

cheap (CHEEP) not wanting to spend money

consequences (KAHN-sih-kwens-iz) punishments or effects

curiosity (kyoor-ee-AH-sih-tee) the need to know something

fables (FAY-buhlz) short stories that teach lessons usually with animals as main characters

housekeeper (HOUS-kee-per) a person whose job is cleaning houses

morals (MOR-uhlz) lessons

obstacle (OB-stuh-kuhl) a thing that blocks a path

proposed (pruh-POHZD) asked to marry

urban legends (UR-buhn LEJ-uhndz) modern stories about people or places that are told like they're true

warriors (WOR-ee-urz) fighters

INDEX